P9-CCJ-333

A GIFT FOR

❖ FROM ❖

FENG SHUI

*How to create harmony and balance
in your living and working environment*

*Text: Belinda Henwood
Consultant: Howard Choy*

Hallmark
BOOKS

STOREY
BOOKS

BOK5017

CONTENTS

Relationships

Fame

Prosperity

The Basis of Feng Shui

What is Feng Shui?

FENG SHUI (PRONOUNCED "FOONG SWEE" IN CANTONESE AND "FONG SHWEE" IN MANDARIN) IS A WAY OF CREATING HARMONY BETWEEN HUMANS AND OUR ENVIRONMENT TO ENHANCE OUR WELL-BEING. AN ANCIENT CHINESE THEORY OF DESIGN AND PLACEMENT, FENG SHUI GREW FROM OBSERVATIONS THAT PEOPLE ARE AFFECTED — EITHER POSITIVELY OR NEGATIVELY — BY THEIR SURROUNDINGS, WITH SOME PLACES BEING NOTICEABLY LUCKIER, HAPPIER, HEALTHIER OR MORE PEACEFUL THAN OTHERS.

In your home, good feng shui helps create harmonious family relationships, fosters good health, revives energy and enthusiasm and even encourages fertility. In business it attracts prosperity and success. By changing your surroundings feng shui allows you to change your life for the better.

Because there are many elements contributing to your environment, applying feng shui may seem like a complicated business, but there are some basic, time-honored remedies which won't involve you in any great expense or effort. In some cases, feng shui can be as simple as moving furniture around, changing the colors of your decor, hanging wind chimes and mirrors, or placing leafy green plants at your home's entrance.

As you start to adopt the principles of feng shui you will begin to feel the difference. Described as the art of place-ment, feng shui is largely common sense and good design. It is important you take the time to listen to your intuition about what feels right and wrong rather than what you think is right because each situation is different and there is no strict, foolproof formula for you to apply.

How it Works

A feng shui expert would take into consideration the many different elements affecting your environment. For example, they would look at how the energy or qi (chi) moves around your home; the position of your house; its surroundings; the shape of the land; the shape of your house; the directions your rooms face – north, south, east or west; the location of each room – whether they are at the front, back or center; the shapes of your furniture and its placement; the decor of your home as well as the landscaping in your garden. They would also look at each of these in terms of the balance of yin or yang and whether they are associated with the element of earth, fire, metal, water or wood.

All this may sound overwhelming but you don't have to become a feng shui expert overnight. You can take small steps. This book introduces you to the basic concepts behind feng shui and gives you some general "cures". There are also two simple formulas to choose from – the bagua (pages 62–63) or mingua (pages 64–66) – which you can apply to your own home to balance your particular problem areas. Sometimes major changes are suggested but there are also less dramatic alternatives to pursue.

Remember, the remedies you use are likely to have different effects – some will have more impact than others. Installing a window or skylight, for example, in a windowless room will have more effect than placing a mirror there. The window is a physical solution while the mirror is considered a "psychological" cure because it affects your perceptions and therefore your feelings about the place.

Qi or Life Force

Many cultures believe that a universal energy – sometimes called qi (chi) in China, prana (prahna) in India or ki (ki) in Japan – flows constantly through all life forms. This energy or qi flows through the universe and the earth in the same way that it flows through the human body, and changes made by nature or humankind will vary its course. Just as acupuncture, chakra balancing or shiatsu massage can adjust the flow of energy in the body, so can feng shui adjust the flow of energy around us.

Feng shui literally means (the flow of) "wind" and "water". The wind disperses the invisible life energy and the water contains it. When you practice feng shui you attract and cultivate positive energy or sheng qi (shung chi) and dispel or eliminate negative energy or sha qi (shar chi).

The Flow of Qi

Positive sheng qi meanders gently along curved lines while negative sha qi strikes quickly in straight lines. For the qi to be beneficial and nourishing, you need to make sure it keeps flowing – not too quickly and not too slowly. Sheng qi comes from nature while corners, known as "secret arrows", generate sha qi.

Qi should be encouraged to enter a dwelling and its garden and to flow freely and slowly throughout the space. If it is blocked, it will become stagnant and destructive.

As a simple exercise, walk from the front gate, though your home and garden to the back fence and try to imagine how the qi flows.

Qi should flow smoothly and easily through your garden and house.

HEAVEN QI

Planetary Qi
- *universal qi*
- *astrology*
- *sun, moon, planets*
- *cycles of change*
- *spiritual guidance*

Weather Qi
- *sunlight*
- *clouds and rain*
- *wind*
- *seasons*
- *tide*
- *heat and cold*

EARTH QI

Natural Qi
- *vegetation*
- *land forms*
- *mountains*
- *valleys and plains*
- *rivers and the sea*
- *magnetic fields*
- *earth energies*
- *latitude & longitude*

Human Made Qi
- *external built environment*
- *internal environment*
- *interior design, layout and proportions*
- *color, light and sound*

HUMAN QI

Social Qi
- *political and cultural*
- *social contacts*
- *neighbors*
- *partner, family or relatives*
- *local events*

Personal Qi
- *memories and visions*
- *ideals and beliefs*
- *personality and integrity*
- *sensitivity*
- *health and life force*

Heaven, Earth and Human Qi

In heaven there is tien qi (tian chi) or heaven qi, on earth there is di qi (te chi) or earth qi, and in us there is ren qi (ren chi) or human qi. Heaven qi is made up of the forces that heavenly bodies exert on earth such as sun and rain. Earth qi is affected by heaven qi – too much rain will cause flooding, too little will cause plants to die – and then, within the earth qi, each person has his or her own individual qi. The aim of feng shui is to keep harmony and balance between heaven, earth and human qi.

The Three Gifts

Feng shui is also referred to as the study of the way of heaven and earth in relation to humans. It can help us choose a way of life and a place to live that is in harmony with our ren tao (ren dao) or the way of being human. The Chinese call this relationship san cai (san chie) or the three gifts.

Yin and Yang

The Chinese believe everything that exists has qi and, in turn, everything that has qi has yin (passive, feminine) qualities and yang (active, masculine) qualities. Yin and yang are opposites and complementary – one cannot exist without the other. Night does not exist without day, winter without summer, nor shadow without the sun. Similarly, each quality contains some of its opposite. When we feel good about a place the Chinese would say it has good feng shui because the yin and the yang are balanced.

The Tao

The ancient Chinese focused their interest on the relationship between things and their apparent qualities. The theories of yin and yang, the five elements and the eight trigrams formed the basic models to define the relationship of the parts within the whole – the Tao (dao) or the "way".

		YIN	YANG
IDEAS OF		*cold*	*hot*
		dark	*bright*
		soft	*hard*
		heavy	*light*
		wet	*dry*
ASPECTS OF		*femaleness*	*maleness*
		youth	*age*
		negative	*positive*
		passive	*active*
REPRESENTED BY		*earth*	*heaven*
		broken line	*unbroken line*
		tiger	*dragon*
		valley	*mountain*
ESSENCE		*body*	*soul*
DIRECTIONS		*below*	*above*
		down	*up*
		right	*left*
		back	*front*
		in	*out*
NUMBERS		*even*	*odd*
COLORS		*cool blues/greens*	*warm red tones*
ARCHITECTURE		*empty space*	*solid structure*
		curved	*geometric*

The Five Elements

The Chinese believe everything is in a constant state of change between the five elements or forces of nature called wu-xing (woo-shing):

- wood or mu (moo)
- fire or huo (hor)
- earth or t'u (too)
- metal or jin (chin)
- water or shui (shwee)

These aren't literally elements but are qualities, constantly overcoming each other in a continuous cycle. It can be a **creative and productive** relationship: wood fuels fire; fire burns to ash or earth; earth gives minerals or metal; when heated, metal flows like water; and water nourishes wood.

The **destructive and negative** relationship: wood takes nutrients from the earth; earth pollutes or absorbs water; water kills fire; fire melts metal; and metal chops wood.

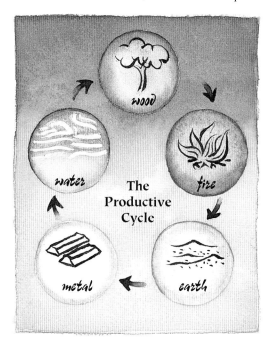

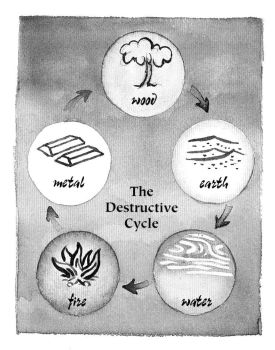

Elements in the Home

For harmony and good feng shui the relationship between the elements needs to be productive. For instance, a child's nursery is associated with the element wood which symbolizes life, growth, creativity and organic material. It is productively linked to fire which is stimulating and will encourage growth. An example of a destructive relationship or bad feng shui is to have the bathroom, associated with the element water, in the center of your home which is associated with earth because earth absorbs water.

Each of the elements is associated with a direction, and the fifth, earth, is associated with the center. Each also has corresponding shapes and colors.

Element	Direction	Shape		Color
WATER	North	∿	wavy	black
FIRE	South	╱╲	pointed	red
WOOD	East	⌒	tall and slender	blue/green
METAL	West	⌢	rounded	white
EARTH	Center	⌐	square and boxed	yellow

The five elements and their associated directions, shapes and colours.

Applying Feng Shui

Feng Shui Tools

YOU WILL FIND AS YOU MOVE INTO THE WORLD OF FENG SHUI THAT THERE ISN'T ONE SIMPLE SYSTEM TO APPLY. OVER THE CENTURIES DIFFERENT SCHOOLS HAVE DEVELOPED. THE FORM SCHOOL, FOR INSTANCE, RELIES ON A GREAT DEAL OF INTUITIVE INSIGHT, AND PLACES EMPHASIS ON THE SHAPE AND CONTOURS OF THE LANDSCAPE. THE COMPASS SCHOOL IS MORE CONCERNED WITH THE MAGNETIC EFFECT OF THE EARTH'S GRAVITATIONAL FIELDS – THE MOVEMENT OF QI – AND UTILIZES THE EIGHT TRIGRAMS OF THE *I CHING* OR *BOOK OF CHANGES*.

Solutions within these schools vary too. Within the Compass School, some people use a compass to find their ideal orientations; some use a bagua to determine the health, relationships or career corners of their homes; while others calculate their personal lucky and unlucky areas according to their birth dates. Each of these systems helps you work out which parts of your home need to be balanced. Later in this book we show you how to use the bagua as well as how to find your own lucky and unlucky directions so you can balance your own home.

You will find, too, when you look at different approaches that the compass, bagua and luo-shu are interchangeable in terms of their shapes – they are merely different ways of depicting the eight compass directions of north, northeast, east, southeast, south, southwest, west, northwest and the areas of life these directions govern.

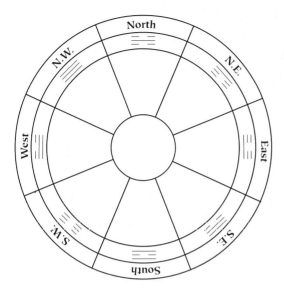

The compass.

The eight trigram bagua.

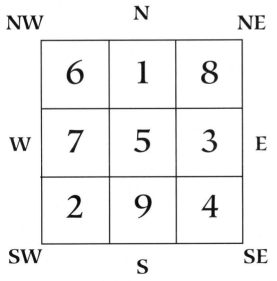

The Luo-shu or 'magic square'.

The Ideal Site

The ideal feng shui site is said to be where the descending heaven qi meets the ascending earth qi. There is no hard and fast rule about the perfect site but there are some general conditions you can look for. Generally, halfway up a hill facing the sun is considered good feng shui because you will have a distant view and you'll get cool summer breezes and warm winter ones.

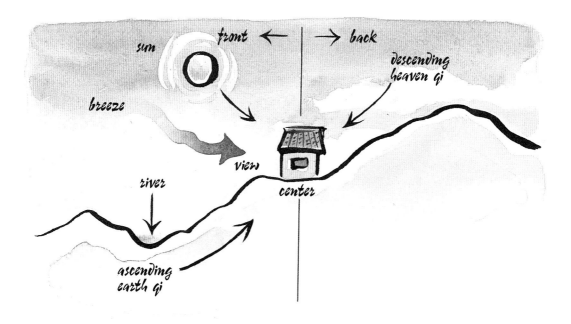

The ideal site for a house.

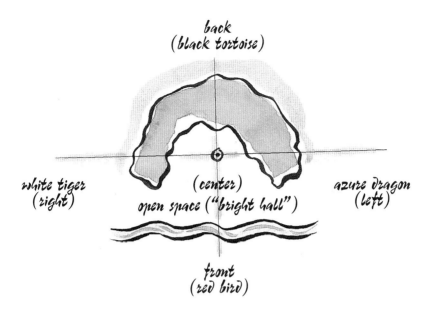

The ideal position for a house.

The Ideal Spot

The ideal feng shui spot for a house is called the xue (shu). It has an open space in front, the "bright hall" or ming tang, with four mythical animals or spirits surrounding it. The red bird is the distant front view; the black tortoise is the protective hill at the back; the azure dragon is to the left and the white tiger to the right. Ideally you should have a stream flowing across in front of the site because water is regarded as a source of food and means of transportation. It is also believed that the heaven qi descends down the hill and is contained by the water.

You will find that the idea of this protective, armchair shape can be applied not only to the site of your home but to the feng shui of a particular room, where chairs are placed so that backs are protected and there is open space in front of you, or to your garden, where you can plant protective trees at the back if there isn't a hill. After all, feeling safe and secure is a large part of being happy.

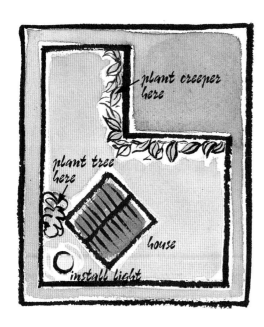

Balance an L-shaped block of land using plants and lighting.

Shape

The shape of your block of land, your house, your rooms, and even your furniture, play an important part in the feng shui of your home. Symmetrical shapes are considered ideal – an L-shape, for instance, poses problems because it is incomplete and unbalanced. When you have irregular shapes, you need to look at how you can balance them.

The Shape of Your Land

A rectangular block of land, wider on the northern and southern ends, is considered to have the best feng shui. If your block isn't a true rectangle, then it is better if the back is wider than the front.

There are a number of ways to balance your block of land.

- Put a lamp or plant a tree in the opposite corner if a corner juts into your land.
- Plant a creeper or hedge around the offending corner to counter any negative energy (sha qi) it might be generating.
- Make sure you fill out the corners of a triangular plot so the qi doesn't get trapped there.

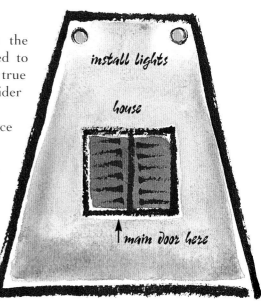

Fill out a triangular block of land by installing light or planting trees in the corners.

The Shape of Your Home

Square or rectangular homes are thought to be most beneficial because homes that are of an irregular shape leave rooms "dangling" outside the flow of qi.

If you have an L-shaped house you can fill out the missing corner by:

- planting a tree or shrub
- using a lamp or spotlight
- building a conservatory or patio.

If you have an L-shaped apartment and can't fill out the corner, try installing a light, or hanging wind chimes or a mirror to square the L.

The Shape of Rooms

In the rooms of your home, square or rectangular shapes, too, will encourage a better flow of qi. An irregular shape will inevitably create a corner that can generate secret arrows of negative sha qi. Here, try pot plants for protection.

If you have an L-shaped living/dining room it is important to create two contained spaces – by using a screen, partition or bookshelves – so that you have two complete rooms.

Furnishings

Again, symmetry is important when it comes to your home's decor. Whether you are choosing a table or a tiny faceted glass crystal think about whether its shape is balanced.

Generally speaking, the shape of the furniture should reflect the shape of the room. For example, if you have a square room use a square, round, or octagonal table. If it is a rectangular room, use a rectangular table, unless it's in the dining room where a round table is often best.

Finding the Center

To determine whether the orientation of your house is auspicious for you, you need to work out where the center of your home is.

The method called li ji (lee jee) can be done in a number of ways, depending on the shape of your house.

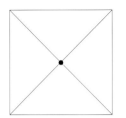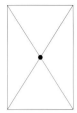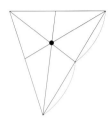

When you have a square, rectangular or triangular house, draw the diagonals and plot the center.

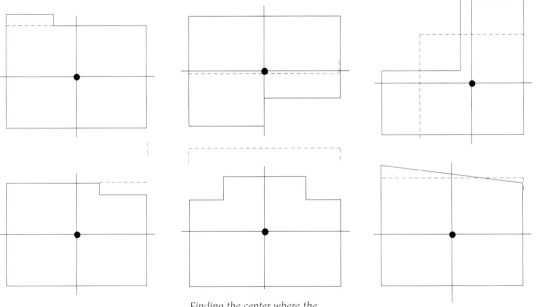

Where there is a minor projection or indentation, you can ignore it.

Finding the center where the projection or indentation of the floor plan is less than half the length or width of the building.

Finding the center of some irregular-shaped buildings.

Finding the Front

While there is always a front and back to a house –
the front with an open space or ming tang facing
the red bird and the back protected by the black
tortoise – the front door is not always where it
seems. The front of your home is where the energy
enters your house. It is the door most often used by
your visitors. In some cases a formal front door is
rarely used and both family and guests find it more
convenient to come into the house through a back
or side door. If this is the case, then consider this
door as your front door.

*Y*our Home

Your Location

STREETS CHANNEL QI JUST AS CORRIDORS AND PAVEMENTS DO AND THE SPEED WITH WHICH IT TRAVELS ALONG THEM DEPENDS ON THE STREETSCAPE AS WELL AS HOW MUCH ACTIVITY THERE IS. BUSY ROADS, BUSTLING WITH TRAFFIC, WILL HAVE FASTER MOVING QI THAN QUIETLY CURVING COUNTRY LANES.

There are a few basic situations to avoid.

- Your front door should not directly face a church, temple, cemetery or railway because the qi will be too concentrated.
- A narrow gap between two buildings can suck nourishing sheng qi (positive energy) from your home.
- A front door facing onto a T-junction or at the end of a cul-de-sac allows qi to flow too quickly towards you; it also means, from a practical point of view, that headlights will shine straight into your home.
- Living near a large freeway will make qi flash past rather than stop awhile to nourish land, buildings and people.

- You need peace and quiet so avoid land under flight paths, next to railway lines, factories or on major roads.
- Your front door should not be close to either end of a bridge. The energy comes from many directions and becomes concentrated at these points, preventing relaxation.

Balancing Unhappy Locations

- Plants, shrubs, or a wall will slow down and screen your home from negative sha qi.
- For added protection you can place a small mirror on the front wall of your house or install a weather vane.
- If you live in an apartment, decorate your balcony with hanging pots.
- Fences and walls also benefit from living things – try growing creepers over them to enhance the qi.
- The sound of water or chimes will help reduce unwanted noise.

The Entrance

The front door is regarded by the Chinese as the "mouth" of the home because this is where the external qi – the energy from the environment – comes into your house. It is vital, therefore, that the position of the front door encourages beneficial sheng qi and discourages destructive sha qi. An entry porch or front verandah, or even an overhang, creates a better qi mouth, helping to draw in the energy.

Following principles of good design, the front door should be in proportion to the rest of your home. Too large a door or "mouth" will let qi out, too narrow won't let it in.

No matter what the scale of the house, the front door should always be unpretentious and practical, otherwise you will invite trouble into your home. A big "mouth" can also give people the wrong impression.

Ideally your front door should face the warmth of the sun so you can capture fame, fortune and longevity. If your front door is on the yin or sunless side, hang wind chimes near it to stimulate positive sheng qi.

Both people and positive qi will be attracted by a welcoming entrance:

- *always keep the front door in good repair*
- *remove any clutter or untidiness*
- *make sure the lighting is good, and*
- *keep a porch light on at night, even while you are away.*

A Place of Transition

Both the Chinese and Japanese have a tradition of having a place of transition – between the outside world and their personal space – at the entrance to their homes. A place to stop, sit down and take off your shoes. This not only requires you to change direction before you move inside but it means the positive sheng qi can flow around and inside while the negative sha qi (traveling in straight lines) is stopped.

Once inside the door, your home should be as welcoming as the approach. Dark, narrow entrances won't encourage either people or nourishing sheng qi and walls opposite an entrance will obstruct it. You can open up the space, however, by hanging a picture, especially a landscape, and warm, soft lighting will help.

A clear view from your front door straight through to the garden isn't good feng shui because it is considered impolite to show guests the back door as soon as they arrive. Also, a front door directly facing a back door means that the qi will run straight through without having a chance to move around your home bringing you prosperity and opportunity. A crystal or wind chimes hanging just inside the front door will help remedy the situation, although you'll find a folding screen or a small wall will slow the flow of qi down more effectively.

The Living Room

A living room needs to be warm and welcoming – a happy place in which to entertain and for your family to gather together. Whatever style of decor you choose – formal, casual, traditional or contemporary – your living room will affect your friendships, family relationships and your success.

The most public part of your home, the living room is the most lively room so the qi needs to flow in a lively fashion. It is a yang room so take care to add some touches of yin softness such as scatter cushions, and coolness, like leafy, green plants.

The best orientation is the one that will capture the most sun (south-facing in the northern hemisphere and north-facing in the southern hemisphere), with an easterly aspect for a family who likes to get up early in the morning and a westerly aspect for one who likes to stay up late.

Balancing the Orientation

If your living room doesn't have the ideal orientation, adjust the feng shui by other means:

- bright, cheerful colors will make it more lively
- a fish tank will add a restful focal point while the movement of the colorful goldfish will help stimulate qi.

Furniture

The shape and size of the furniture in your living room should reflect the size and shape of the room. If the pieces are too large the flow of qi will be disrupted causing you to feel uncomfortable. If you have a square-shaped room, use a square, round, or octagonal table. If the room is rectangular, use a rectangular table.

Correct placement of living room furniture allows qi to flow freely.

How you position your furniture will have an enormous effect on how well your living room works.

- Where possible, place furniture against the four walls. Avoid placing chairs in a position that puts the occupier's back to a full length window or door because it will make them feel insecure.
- Chairs should be positioned to encourage a free flow of movement – for people and qi – as well as conversation.
- Take care not to place chairs between two opposite openings. The qi generated by your family's passing parade will interfere with conversation and you'll lose both concentration and your temper. You can put them to the side of the qi channel, encouraging a flow of qi rather than disrupting it.
- Sitting face to face can be confronting so slightly angle chairs to the side.
- A shared table between chairs will help break down barriers between people.
- Don't place chairs under exposed beams because the person seated beneath will find it oppressive. If it can't be avoided, hang a pair of bamboo flutes from the beam.

The Bedroom

The happiness of a marriage, the quality of sex and the health and wealth of a couple can be affected by the feng shui of the bedroom. It is where we spend approximately one third of our lives – sleeping, which is also when we are at our most vulnerable.

A bedroom is a very private place where you recharge your batteries and regain physical and spiritual strength so it should be peaceful, secure and subdued. It should also reflect who you are, otherwise you won't reach a state of complete relaxation.

The best orientation for a bedroom is away from the hot sun – to the east for the young and active and to the west for the elderly. A bedroom is best away from traffic noise and not near a kitchen, bathroom or store room unless they are well ventilated because the stagnant qi they foster can cause health problems. Build a protective partition if need be.

The ceiling should not be too high or too low – cathedral ceilings are considered too high and less than eight feet (2.5 m) is probably too low. A low slanting ceiling or beams aren't good over a bed because their angles direct negative sha qi and can cause headaches, illness or confusion. Also, an overhead beam that divides the bed of a married couple can cause disagreement.

Remember to take care that the sharp edges of wardrobes, bookshelves or the walls of an irregularly shaped room are covered otherwise the result could be minor health problems or irritability.

With the bed positioned diagonally opposite the doorway, energy can flow freely and you are protected from drafts and disturbance.

The Bed

Positioning the bed is your most important task for good feng shui in the bedroom.

- Don't have the foot of the bed in line with the door. (In many cultures it is believed that the dead should be laid out with their feet pointing towards the door to allow them easier access to heaven.)
- The best place is in the area of assembled qi – usually diagonally opposite the door. (Directly opposite or near the door is known as the area of disturbed qi.)
- Don't have your head in line with the bedroom door – it will make you restless.
- A view of the door is good, but you should be some distance from it.
- The bed head should be against a solid wall.
- If the bed must be near a window, leave space for a small table or chair. Also, qi can escape through windows at night so make sure curtains or blinds are closed.
- Make sure your bed isn't in a crosscurrent between the door and the window.
- Some say that the bed head should be on the north/south axis so that you are in line with the magnetic energy of the earth.

Mirrors

One mirror in the bedroom is considered enough and it definitely shouldn't face the bed because it can cause restlessness – the Chinese believe your spirit will get a nasty shock in the night when it sees its own reflection. If it's fun you're after and not sleep, mirrored ceilings and walls in the bedroom are the answer – they are far from restful because they make qi bounce all over the place.

Balancing your bedroom

- *If you can't avoid having your feet pointing towards the door when you're in bed, hang a crystal or wind chimes between the bed and the entrance to disperse the negative sha qi. If there's enough space, place a folding screen between the bed and the door.*
- *Hang two bamboo flutes pointing upwards on an exposed beam or a sloping ceiling. Also, make sure the length of your bed is under the slope or the beam.*
- *A crystal hanging from the ceiling between sharp corners and your bed will interrupt the secret arrows of destructive sha qi. Also, plants and screens will slow down their flow.*

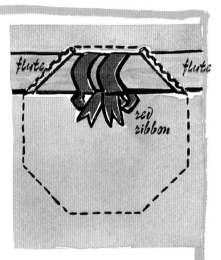

Flutes are placed as though they are a part of the octagonal bagua shape, with the mouthpieces pointing down.

Electronic Equipment

It is always nice to curl up in bed and watch some television, or retreat to the bedroom to work on your computer but this isn't the ideal place to keep electronic equipment. If you do keep a TV or computer screen in the bedroom, cover them at night with an opaque cloth so they won't act as mirrors.

Baby's Bedroom

The nurturing nursery is best positioned on the eastern or southeastern (in the northern hemisphere) or northeastern (in the southern hemisphere) side of your home. The soft, warm rays of the rising sun and ascending yang will give your baby life-giving qi.

A child's room should be connected with nature.

- Have direct access into the garden or a view of plants and shrubs or, if these aren't possible, use indoor plants to create the necessary sheng qi for growth.
- Use light shades of green in the room, even if it is only in accents like a piece of furniture or a mobile.
- Line the walls and floors with natural materials like wallpaper or wood paneling, and use wool carpet and soft, organic furnishings. Avoid plastics if you can.

Take into account the sex of your baby, too. Boys are yang so they'll benefit from the balance of cool yin blues in decoration, while girls are yin and require warm, red yang tones.

A rectangular room is best, close to the parents' room and away from noise. Natural light and good ventilation are important but if the nursery is dark, hang a mobile or wind chimes outside the window.

Baby needs room to grow and the qi space to flow, so keep furniture to a minimum and avoid clutter. And, most importantly of all, for a soundly sleeping baby, place the cot in a secure position, protected by walls and away from doorways and windows.

A Place for the Heart

Every home needs a place where the family gathers together and shares their time – where the human energy or ren qi (ren chi) can be focused and nourished. These days it is often the family room – attached to the kitchen and opening onto the back garden – but it can be a dining room, eat-in kitchen or living room, particularly in winter if there's the warm welcome of a fireplace. Giving your home a healthy and happy heart will bring harmony and prosperity to your family life.

The Family Room

The hub of the modern day home, it is essential the qi flows freely in your family room and has easy access to the rest of your house. With its central location it is associated with the earth element and the color yellow, and because of its lively function the family room is yang.

The best orientation is where the room can capture the sun's warmth for the better part of the day – toward the south or southeast in the northern hemisphere or the north or northeast in the southern hemisphere. If the family room lies on the less sunny side of the house, make sure you have plenty of light – hooded windows or a skylight will help – but if your family room is affected by the strong western sun, protect it with awnings, blinds or a pretty pergola.

If possible, have your family room open out onto a garden or courtyard – this will increase the flow of qi and allow the family to easily flow outside in warm weather.

The Dining Room

The Chinese believe you should not be distracted from the food or the company during a meal because eating feeds both the body and spirit. So, don't make your dining room decor too eye-catching.

If the dining room and kitchen are too near the front door it is said that the family will be preoccupied with eating, and also that guests will eat and run. If attached to the family room, living room or kitchen, make your dining room a separate space by using plants or screens to block distractions. Two doorways will let qi flow in and out but, if there's only one, allow enough space around it for easy access.

Table and chairs for health and happiness

- Chairs should be comfortable so diners take their time to eat, digest well, and communicate with each other.
- Ideally, chairs should have good back rests and arms – the "armchair" shape of the four animal spirits.
- Place chairs with their backs to the wall rather than to the windows and doors.
- Dining chairs should be even in number because even numbers represent luck and single chairs loneliness. Add an extra chair if you have an uneven number.
- A round table is best. The next choice is octagonal and, if you have a square or rectangular table make sure no one gets a corner! The negative sha qi could cause digestive problems or bad temper.

The Kitchen

The kitchen is regarded as the source of general well-being by the Chinese because food represents wealth. If you prepare food in a kitchen with good feng shui the people who eat it will carry the benefits throughout the day.

Your kitchen is best placed to one side of your home – preferably on the south or southeastern side in the northern hemisphere and the north or northeastern side in the southern hemisphere – and not in the center which is associated with the earth element. Nor should it be too close to the front door. It is considered bad luck to have the kitchen facing the front door and too close to the bathroom is unhygienic.

The balance of yang and yin is vital here where the two major elements are fire (yang) and water (yin). Your kitchen should be light and airy with little clutter. Choose smooth surfaces – preferably lighter shades – and always keep your kitchen clean. You will find indoor plants, window boxes, or small shrubs outside the window will help it stay cool.

The area around the kitchen door or directly opposite is known as the area of disturbed qi and isn't a good place to put your stove. Rather, place it where there is assembled qi – diagonally across from the door.

Happy cooking, healthy bank balance

- The stove next to the sink or refrigerator isn't good planning as it is not desirable to have fire and water side by side. If your kitchen design doesn't allow another option, put a buffer – a metal or wooden partition, even a chopping board – between the two.
- Be careful water pipes are not placed under the stove.
- For good feng shui it is considered best to position the stove towards the east and the southeast of your kitchen because it belongs to the wood element. Other possibilities are the northeast (earth) or the south (fire).
- Place the stove so your back isn't to the door while cooking, otherwise you may be surprised by someone coming up behind you and this could affect the food. If you can't see the door, install a mirror behind the burners – to give you plenty of warning, to open up the kitchen, to help the flow of qi, but also to bring you good fortune in business.
- Always keep the stove clean and the burners in good working order. It is not only hygienic but is good for business.
- The stove should not be placed under a window or skylight, because the energy will quickly leave the house.
- It is considered bad luck if you can see your stove from the front door.
- Use all the burners regularly to keep the energy flowing evenly and to maximize your income potential.

The Bathroom

The Chinese have a saying: "A clean and beautiful bathroom is the key to health, peace, and wealth" but it's not quite as simple as that. The bathroom poses an interesting problem because the basic element – water – plays two roles. It represents money and it washes away dirt. This means that every time you flush water down your drains you are in danger of sending your family's fortunes with it.

Your bathroom should be spacious enough to be functional but not too large. It should be a retreat – a place where you can relax and pamper yourself. Pale colors are restful – green promotes digestion and aids health; blue will keep the water moving, help avoid plumbing problems, and encourage a good cash flow.

Associated with the element water, the bathroom shouldn't be next to the fire of the kitchen (because water destroys fire). Nor should it be in the middle of the home which is associated with earth (earth destroys water by absorbing it).

Ideally, too, the bathroom and toilet should be separate because they serve different functions – one is for external cleansing, the other for internal. Each needs a window to keep the air fresh and to connect the room to the outside.

Balancing Your Bathroom

- If your bathroom faces or is above the front door, place a small mirror at the base of the toilet to stop the qi and the family's wealth from going down the drain.
- If it is next to or above the kitchen, hang a mirror outside the door to deflect negative energy.
- The bathroom should not be in the center of the home because it is associated with harmony and long life and should not have a utilitarian purpose. If it is in the center, hang mirrors in your bathroom or install a ventilated skylight.
- Colored ribbons and wind chimes near artificial ventilation devices will flutter and make music and enliven qi.
- The most yin room in the house, the bathroom is often damp and dark so add yang for balance – some bright splashes of color or lighted candles.
- Keep drains covered as much as possible and the toilet seat closed when not in use. If you flush the toilet with the lid open, chances are your money will go too.
- If the toilet is located in the bathroom, it should not be visible from the doorway. Behind the door or in an alcove is best, or a screen, curtain or cabinet can shield it from view.
- Use green indoor plants to help activate stagnant qi.

The Home Office

Whether you work from home or simply have a study or work station, you need to take care to separate its activity from your home life because each has a different pattern of qi. Ideally you should have a completely separate entrance into your home office so you can more easily move from one mode into another and close the door on your work at the end of the day.

Unfortunately, most of us have to steal some space from the family room or even the bedroom for our "offices". Then, it is most important to do what you can, both physically and mentally, to keep these two parts of your life distinct.

• Make a clear division with a screen, bookshelves, or cupboards to hide your office from view.
• If your office is in your bedroom you need to pay particular attention to very different requirements of the yin aspect of the room to rest and sleep and the yang aspect to be alert while you work.
• If you have a computer screen in the bedroom, cover it at night so that it won't act as a mirror and disturb your spirit while you sleep.
• Make a threshold into your office with a floor rug or potted plants.
• Create a routine like walking out of the house in the morning to get the newspaper – so you can read it at morning tea – and coming back in to sit down to work. Don't forget, too, to leave your office at the end of the day!

Electrical Equipment
It is important to think about balance when it comes to electrical equipment as electricity can stimulate qi. These days we are surrounded by electrical devices in our homes – from household appliances to computers, televisions, stereos and even heating and cooling equipment so pay attention to settling their effect. Conceal equipment in cabinets or closets or cover with a beautiful cloth when not in use.

Good Qi for Work

The qi in your home office or study needs the balance of calm and quiet along with being mentally stimulating. You will want yin or cool hues to help concentration and gentle lighting with an orientation towards the east – the rising sun brings you yang qi which is beneficial for thinking and reading.

If your home office is situated to the west of the house, the strong setting sun will make you feel sleepy so you'll need devices to control the heat and glare. For practical reasons it is preferable if you are away from the activity and noise of the kitchen or family room.

The qi from a window can distract you from your work so make sure your desk isn't placed directly underneath. Put it in a secure corner if you can, with your back against a wall and so you can easily see the doorway. Lighting should come from the side of your desk – left if you are right-handed and right if you are left-handed.

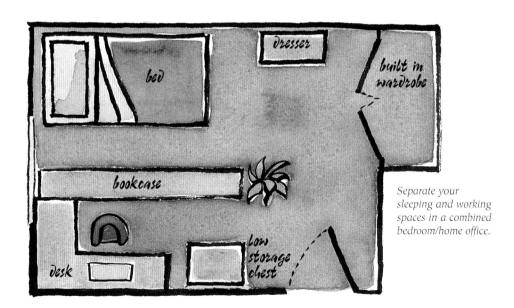

Separate your sleeping and working spaces in a combined bedroom/home office.

Internal Features

Windows

*T*HINK OF THE WINDOWS AS THE EYES AND NOSE OF YOUR HOME, OPENINGS THAT ALLOW YOU TO LOOK OUT AND, AT THE SAME TIME, TAKE IN THE QI BREATH OR VITAL ENERGY. WINDOWS ALSO LET IN WELCOME WARMTH AND SUNSHINE OR YANG QI. IF YOU HAVE A ROOM THAT HAS TOO MUCH YIN AND IS DARK AND DINGY, INSTALL AN EXTRA WINDOW, MAKE AN EXISTING ONE LARGER IF YOU CAN, OR FIT A SKYLIGHT.

If this isn't possible you can introduce other yang influences such as mirrors to enlarge the space, and remedies such as bright colors, lights, crystals, flowers and plants, to enliven the qi (see CURES pages 54–61).

Windows help the healthy circulation of fresh air and qi and they should be relatively tall and wide to provide a generous flow. If necessary, you can regulate the flow with blinds, drapes, curtains or shutters depending on the location, function and orientation of your room.

Where possible have two opening windows in a room. From a practical point of view this creates cross-ventilation and a more even distribution of natural light but it also means there is less chance of qi stagnating.

Windows as protection

• *If you feel your neighbors are looking in on you, chances are that you won't feel comfortable with them – or friendly. Privacy is vital to a sense of well-being so make sure your window coverings, plants, or ornaments screen the inside of your home.*

• *If secret arrows of negative sha qi are being directed into your home from outside influences – like rooftops, corners of buildings or lampposts – place a plant, vase, or statue on your windowsill to help prevent them from entering.*

The Importance of Views

A good view is good feng shui. A good view not only increases the value of a property but the beneficial sheng qi it brings encourages good luck and prosperity.

- A blank wall outside your window will generate negative sha qi so plant some shrubs, put in window boxes or place a planter on the sill, filled with cheery flowers.
- If you aren't lucky enough to have a pleasing view you can improve the feng shui by paying special attention to your window dressing. Pretty drapes, curtains, swags and other decorating details will help detract from a gloomy outlook.

Feng Shui Sayings

There is an old feng shui saying that if your house doesn't have an overhang on the south-facing windows (north-facing in the southern hemisphere) there will be disharmony and domestic arguments. While this may sound far-fetched, it makes some sense. A room that isn't protected from the hot sun will soon become stuffy and the inhabitants are likely to be bad-tempered.

It is also said that if you open the north-facing windows (south-facing in the southern hemisphere) it will affect a woman's menstrual cycle. Again, this is not so strange. A room on the sunless side of the house will tend to be cold and damp and if you open the windows you let in even more yin energy. A woman is yin by nature and particularly so during menstruation so she will need the yang energy of sunlight and warmth to make her feel well and balanced.

Doors

While the front door is the "mouth" of the house that allows nourishing qi or energy to enter, the internal doors and corridors help keep it moving smoothly. Make sure your doors are aligned properly, open and close easily, and are clear of furniture and other constraints.

It is vital that your front door isn't directly opposite the back door because the qi will leave too quickly without having had time to circulate throughout your home. Three aligned doors are also considered bad feng shui – especially if two of them are front and back doors – but a screen, tall plant or beaded curtains or drapes can help. You can also try hanging a crystal, wind chimes or a pair of bamboo flutes above the center door to draw up the negative sha qi.

Doors at the end of long corridors face the problem of fast-moving qi and of reaching a dead end, blocking off opportunities. A mirror hanging on the door may help slow down the qi and open up the space.

The back door of opportunity
The back door is important in feng shui because it represents indirect opportunities. Give these opportunities easy access by having your back door opening on to a wide rather than a narrow pavement and avoid having obstructions directly outside like a brick wall. Large glass doors at the back of your home invite the qi to bring peace and harmony into your home – and then allow it to leave as it pleases.

Stairs

Qi takes the stairs when it travels from one floor to another in your home. To ensure its smooth and easy movement, your stairs should curve gently upwards.

The ideal place for a staircase is at the side of the house and towards the back of the building and it is desirable to have a landing or change of direction halfway up. It is considered bad luck to have your staircase directly opposite your front door because qi and money can run straight down and out of your life.

To help prevent qi from rushing down your stairs and out your front door you can hang:

- drapes or curtains at the bottom of the stairs
- a mirror on the landing to draw the qi up into the house
- wind chimes or a crystal between the last stair and the entrance to help moderate the qi flow.

To help qi upstairs:

- make sure the stairs are well-lit and wide
- put potted plants under the stairs to help the qi rise
- have solid stairs rather than those with spaces between the risers so the qi can't escape through the treads – if you have open treads a mirror face-up under the stairs will help send the qi back up
- for a spiral staircase try hanging wind chimes halfway to slow down the qi
- hang artwork that encourages an upward movement of qi – images or representations that are light and bright like birds in flight.

Fireplaces

A friendly fire easily becomes the focus of a room – or home – in cold weather. Take care, though, that beneficial qi doesn't escape up your chimney, by hanging a mirror above the mantelpiece.

If you use your fireplace often it can create too much fiery energy. Green, leafy plants (associated with the element earth) placed either side of the hearth will help correct the balance but make sure your plants aren't too woody because wood fuels fire.

Beams

Overhead beams can be oppressive – particularly if you are sitting or lying directly underneath. The darker, thicker and lower they are, the more powerful their effect.

To help balance the effect of a beam you can:

- break the pathway of the qi through the beam by hanging two bamboo flutes at angles (to form an octagonal shape) and tied with red ribbons – make sure the mouthpieces are pointing down
- decorate the beam with a piece of fabric, a banner or a swag
- paint it a light color so it appears less heavy
- use the qualities of metal – light colors and round shapes – to complement the element of the beam which is wood.

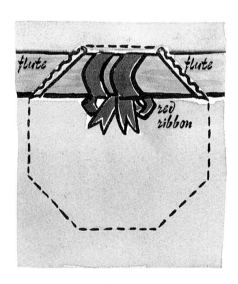

Hang bamboo from beams at angles to form part of the octagonal, bagua shape. Always point the mouthpieces downwards.

Split Levels

If you live in a split-level home or apartment do all you can to make it seem as one level, by using good lighting and wide steps – preferably with plants at the side. If you sleep in a split-level room, make sure you sleep on the upper level. If you have a sunken room, install a light that points upwards to help lift trapped qi.

Corners

When a corner juts into a room you need to soften it to prevent it generating destructive secret arrows of sha qi. Take away their edges by placing plants or sculptures in front.

The empty corners of a room can draw qi in where it tends to stagnate. This is particularly the case if it's where you stash the things that don't have a proper place – like boxes, old magazines, or sporting equipment. Round out corners by placing furniture at a diagonal but then make sure you fill the spaces with lights, plants, baskets or sculptures.

*Y*our Garden

Attracting Qi

WHETHER YOU HAVE A LARGE BACKYARD, A SMALL COURTYARD, SOME POTTED PLANTS ON A BALCONY OR A HUMBLE WINDOW BOX, THE IDEA OF HARMONY APPLIES JUST AS MUCH IN YOUR GARDEN AS IT DOES INSIDE YOUR HOME. AN APPEALING EXTERIOR WILL HELP ATTRACT NOURISHING QI AND WILL IMPROVE YOUR HOME'S OVERALL FENG SHUI.

The most important thing to remember is that although it was made by human hands, your garden should look as though it is the work of Mother Nature. The best advice for the inexperienced feng shui gardener is to keep it simple and natural. Don't go for too many bold, contrasting colors and stick to what grows well in your area, because feng shui plants vary from region to region.

protective planting

Protective Planting

The ideal feng shui site has a hill behind the house to protect the home from cold winds. If there is a hill missing behind you, you can substitute it with trees planted in your garden, but make sure they are healthy evergreens to ensure a beneficial and ongoing effect.

Plan for a Natural Look

Even though you may be wanting to imitate nature it is a good idea to have a plan. Think about how you use your garden and also how it will look from your windows, because that will also affect what is happening inside your home.

- Try to balance the shapes and sizes of plants.
- Don't forget to consider the different shades of green as color in your garden.
- Bright, colorful, flowering plants, like yellow chrysanthemum and bougainvillea, will ward off bad luck.
- Potted cumquat trees near the front door will bring good luck.
- Rocks provide a good contrast to soft plants and help balance the yang with the yin.
- Statues and rockeries should be kept in scale. When there are too many or they are too big they will interfere with the qi flow.
- Climbers – like wisteria, jasmine or clematis – are excellent for covering sharp edges which generate negative sha qi.
- Hollows don't help qi move so build these areas up – perhaps with rockeries.
- The Chinese like fragrant gardens because nourishing sheng qi flows with pleasant scents – plant some honeysuckle, jasmine, clematis, lilac, daphne, gardenias, lavender or roses.
- Take advantage of serenity and space and make some special places for contemplation – fish ponds, a garden bench, a trellis or a sculpture provide positive focal points for quiet thought.
- Quality is better than quantity and, like nature, your garden can be beautiful without being fussy.

Bagua-shaped pavers with thyme growing in between encourage the flow of qi.

Pavements

Build your garden pavements so they encourage positive sheng qi.

- Make a straight pavement seem curved with shrubs, flowers, potted plants, stones or ornaments along one edge.
- The Chinese use mosaic pebbles because their design emphasizes the duality of yin and yang.
- A narrow pavement is better than a wide one – three to four feet (0.9 m to 1.2 m) is wide enough for most houses.
- Low earth mounds on either side of the pavement will create more interest and will also increase the flow of qi.
- Curving pavements enable you to create surprises in your garden.
- With paving, try to avoid straight lines if you can – use a herringbone pattern or a bagua shape.
- Use pavers, rather than solid concrete, because they allow the earth qi to come through as well as letting the water through. Put plants between your pavers – thyme is effective because you can walk on it. Shrubs in pots will also make paving seem friendlier.
- Consider making a private paved area, screened from the house.

Trees

Trees will give your garden protection, especially at the back. However, it is important to consider the shapes of your trees. When you look at Chinese paintings you will notice the softness of the trees – willows, maples, tulip trees and magnolias.

Unless you live in mountainous areas which are the natural home of tall, angular trees like conifers, choose those with gentler shapes.

Cutting down an old tree, particularly one that is weathered and gnarled, can cause problems since the qi will have become used to moving around it, so don't leave an empty space. Break up a straight line of trees by having curved borders underneath.

Hedges and Screens

Use hedges to create secret gardens, but leave them looking natural rather than overpruned. They will be more effective if they can follow curves rather than straight lines.

Brick walls can also be used for screening – again, better curved than straight and their height should be in proportion to the area they surround.

Driveways

Like garden pavements and internal corridors, driveways channel qi. If they narrow towards the front entrance of the house, they concentrate the qi too much; if they get wider, the qi weakens. Ideally, you want a wide curving drive – a horseshoe shape lets the qi arrive and leave easily – with a gentle slope. Too steep a slope and money will disappear so install a light, posts or pillars where the land drops away.

Water

A stream running through your garden is considered to be very good feng shui because moving water attracts qi – it recharges energy and brings a feeling of harmony and balance. While a stream may be a little difficult to organize, you may think about a fountain or a birdbath – particularly placed in the center of a straight pavement.

When you have water in your garden, balance its yin with yang. A nearby rockery, for instance, would balance the rough with the smooth and stillness with movement.

Ponds should have a natural shape – not square or rectangular – and their banks should be sloping. You could add goldfish for prosperity and a tortoise for longevity.

A fountain or stream brings yin to your garden.

Even in a confined space you can encourage qi to meander.

Courtyards and Balconies

No matter how small your garden it can help channel beneficial qi into your home.

In a patio garden or on a balcony you should try to recreate the feeling of a larger garden, using the classic feng shui armchair shape. Shrubs or taller potted plants could represent the black tortoise "hill" at the back, and a pond or fish bowl the water at the front. Placing statues of the four animal spirits – the black tortoise at the back, the azure dragon to the left, the white tiger to the right and a crane or heron in front – will also improve the feng shui.

The protective armchair shape also works in your courtyard: with taller plantings at the back, it should be sheltered from extremes and have access to both sunlight and cool breezes. It needs at least two openings so beneficial sheng qi can enter, move around slowly, then return to nature.

*Y*our Business

Location

*T*HE LOCATION OF A SUCCESSFUL BUSINESS IS QUITE DIFFERENT FROM THAT OF A TRANQUIL HOME ENVIRONMENT. THEY EACH HAVE DIFFERENT PATTERNS OF QI – ONE IS ACTIVE AND THE OTHER PASSIVE, WHICH IS WHY IT CAN BE DIFFICULT TO WORK FROM HOME. BUSY STREETS AND INTERSECTIONS ARE IDEAL FOR BURGEONING BUSINESSES, WHILE OFFICES NEED A QUIETER POSITION THAN A SHOP.

- The less visible your business is from the public, the more you need beneficial qi to help send business your way. You can draw people in by using color and light in eye-catching signs.
- Make the inside of your place of business look attractive and inviting to encourage both customers and qi. Many small businesses make the mistake of filling their windows with signs and information instead of allowing a good, clear view of an appealing interior.

Fish help money come in
You can apply the same feng shui principles of success to your business as you do in your home. Water and fish are good examples. A fountain near the entrance will be good for business and, you may have noticed, in Chinese restaurants there's often a fish tank with goldfish near the cash register – this is to help the money come in.

Offices

- If you have an open plan office, move the desks so they don't directly face each other.
- Long corridors become channels of qi and doors directly opposite each other can create conflict. If there is a window at the end of the corridor it is a good idea to have a blind. Keep your office door closed if it's directly opposite another.
- Square or rectangular offices will bring the most success; you may find it difficult to complete projects in an L-shaped office.
- It is best to make the manager's office the one furthest from the front door so the distractions of people coming and going won't be a problem.

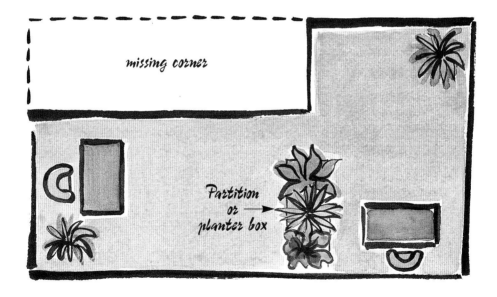

missing corner

Partition or planter box

How to balance an L-shaped office.

Your Workplace

It is hard to imagine anything more removed from nature than most workplaces these days – artificial lighting, computer screens, photocopiers, air that doesn't come in through the windows. It is a challenge to create a sense of natural harmony and balance when you are in a building many floors up in the air. On top of this, the workplace has to fulfill a number of roles for a number of different people and it may not be possible to reorganize it to any great extent.

There are some simple things you can do in your own work space that will help your immediate environment:

- have task lighting if you can
- bring in some green, leafy pot plants or a goldfish bowl for some positive energy
- to avoid the negative influence of sha qi cover any sharp corners pointing towards you with plants or hang small decorations from them
- if you face glare, use a crystal to disperse the qi
- don't hang mobiles, lights or other fixtures directly over your desk
- tidy distracting clutter
- don't place your desk directly under a skylight because it will disperse energy.

Working from home
To run a business successfully from home you need to separate work from family life and if you are starting a new business, you particularly need to keep the energies distinct so that you stay strong and vital. Have your office close to the front door, keeping it away from family life.

Desks

The layout of your working space is basically common sense – your desk should be an appropriate size with adequate storage and working surface. The ideal place for a desk is in the opposite corner to the door, parallel to a wall rather than at an angle and preferably with a solid wall behind.

- Square and rectangular desks are more suitable for making money while oval, round or curved are more conducive to creative work.
- A desk in too strong a color, like black, will make working more difficult.
- If your desk directly faces a door, it may make visitors feel uncomfortable.
- You could find a mirror in front of your desk unsettling and objects hanging behind your head – like diplomas or artwork – will distract your visitors from business.

Sit with your back to a solid wall so you can easily see the door and window. Light coming from a window at the side is desirable.

*C*ures

Feng Shui Cures

*T*HERE ARE TWO BROAD TYPES OF SOLUTIONS IN FENG SHUI — ONE IS "INTO THIS WORLD" OR RUSHI (ROOSHI) AND THE OTHER IS "OUT OF THIS WORLD" OR CHUSHI (CHOOSI). RUSHI CURES WORK ON A PHYSICAL LEVEL, LIKE INSTALLING A WINDOW IN A WINDOWLESS ROOM.

In this chapter you will find the chushi cures – mirrors, crystals, flutes and fish tanks among others – which are a collection of remedies developed through the centuries by feng shui experts. They are regarded as psychological cures because the subtle adjustments they make to your environment come by way of the effect they have on your perceptions.

Sometimes a rushi solution isn't practical or economical and a chushi solution can be used instead. You'll find that often the best remedy for bad feng shui comes with a combination of both rushi and chushi cures.

It is vital to remember that to maximize the power of a chushi cure you need to pay some attention to the space where you use it. Clutter around wind chimes or a mirror won't allow it to fulfill its positive potential.

Aquariums and Goldfish

The word for fish also means "surplus" in Chinese so a fish tank with goldfish could boost your finances because their activity and color can help stimulate qi. The most auspicious numbers of goldfish are three, six, eight or nine.

Bamboo Flutes

Bamboo flutes at an angle to produce an octagonal shape can help direct qi. Most often you find them tied with a red ribbon, fastened to an oppressive beam in a ceiling or to an archway between a front and back door that directly face each other.

Balance your cures
Always keep in mind that you are looking for long-term balance and harmony, so take care not to "overdo" your feng shui cures. Make subtle changes and leave them for a period of time – feel their effect before you try another.

Color

The psychological effects of color are well known. Not only can it make a room seem larger or smaller, warmer or cooler but color can make a room cheerful or depressing.

In feng shui, the compass points have particular colors associated with them. Ideally the main color in a room should be the one that complements the direction it faces. You don't have to use the color in its primary state – you can use tones that are more suited to your personal taste and the particular space.

If, for instance, your bedroom faces east it will catch the warm morning sun no matter what the color of the room. At night you will want the room to be restful so it would be wise to choose the blue/green colors of the east which are also associated with the element wood.

If you find that you don't like the color associated with a particular orientation you can always choose a neutral for the walls and use the feng shui color as accents in soft furnishings or ornaments. Black accents, for example, combine well with natural tones.

Color can also be used as a remedy in feng shui when you aren't physically able to change the layout of a room. For instance, to make the qi flow more slowly in a study you should use quiet yin colors like cool blues and greens.

Rooms facing north in the northern hemisphere and the south in the southern hemisphere will be cool and will benefit from the yang of warm reds; while the south in the northern hemisphere and the north in the southern hemisphere will be warm and are best in cool yin blues and greens.

Direction	Element	Color
North	Water	Black
South	Fire	Red
East	Wood	Blue/Green
West	Metal	White
Center	Earth	Yellow

Crystals

Any object that brings light into an area will activate positive qi. Crystals, lighting, mirrors and even paintings on a wall will enliven a dark spot.

Clear, faceted glass crystals can help activate qi.

- Hang one in the center of a window to bring life into a room.
- Even where there is no window, a crystal will draw qi in.
- It is best to have crystals that are symmetrical in shape – rather than in the shape of an animal, for example – otherwise it could cause imbalance.
- Crystals don't need to be large, unless you have a very large room.
- Try hanging a crystal over the spot where clutter collects.

Indoor Plants

Plants can fill spaces where qi is absent or hide sharp corners that generate the secret arrows of sha qi. Large plants will also slow qi down.

It is important to choose what works well for your local area and to follow your own cultural traditions when it comes to indoor plants. A flourishing plant, not a sick one, improves your feng shui, and what is considered a lucky choice by some cultures may be considered unlucky by others.

Feng shui plants vary from region to region but there are some plants that traditionally are considered to create harmony.

- The impala lily (*Adenium obesum*) is the "flower of wealth and prosperity" and is well placed in your living room or near the front of a shop or business.
- The money plant *(Dracaena)*, an evergreen, brings wealth and long life and is effective in offices and studies.
- Cactus ward off evil spirits.
- The chili plant symbolizes growth and wealth.
- At Chinese New Year the Chinese bring plum blossom into their homes because it represents growth and renewal.
- Indoor plants with red, yellow or orange flowers will add yang colors to a yin room.

Light

Light represents energy and natural light is good feng shui. Artificial lighting can help adjust the qi in dark or difficult spots, but take care that it creates the same stabilizing effect as natural light and that you have a balance between the two.

- Glare from the outside should be softened by drapes, curtains or blinds.
- Harsh overhead lighting can be oppressive whereas table lamps create soft pools of light and make a room feel more relaxed.
- An upward facing floor lamp helps stimulate qi in a dark corner or a sunken room.
- Washing a wall with light brings energy to the area.
- Candles add yang qualities to a yin area.

Use lighting in the garden to:
- balance shape
- even out the surface of the land
- bring life to any dead spots.

Mirrors

The reflective qualities of a mirror can either deflect negative sha qi or encourage positive sheng qi, depending on how you place them around your home. There are three types of mirrors to consider – flat, concave and convex – each with a different reflective quality.

- A convex mirror will diffuse negative sha qi. If you have, for instance, a tall obstruction outside your front door like a tree or lamppost you would be well advised to hang a convex mirror. A flat mirror will also work, but will be less effective than a convex mirror.
- A concave mirror will help attract and absorb beneficial sheng qi into your home. You don't see concave mirrors very often because people usually find other means of encouraging good qi into their homes – through large windows or a welcoming front door.
- A flat mirror has the benefit of providing a perfect mirror image so yin becomes yang and bad qi

becomes good. If you feel the need, you can invest in a special feng shui mirror. These are inexpensive and can be purchased from Chinese stationery shops in your local Chinatown.

Best positions to hang a mirror

- Where it can reflect a pleasant scene from outside – for instance, you would reflect a green tree but not a brick wall.
- At a potentially dangerous spot to deflect the sha qi back on itself – a good example would be above your front door if you live at the end of a cul-de-sac.
- In a windowless or enclosed room such as a bathroom.

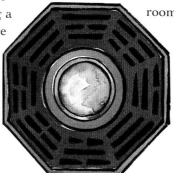

A feng shui mirror

Movement

Things that move in the wind like colored ribbons and weather vanes can also stimulate positive qi or deflect negative qi. Ribbons tied to an artificial ventilation system in a bathroom will get qi moving while a weather vane on the roof of your home will help discourage sha qi that is directed towards you from a neighboring building.

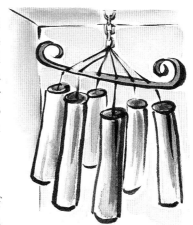

Solid Objects

Large, heavy objects can help create a sense of stillness – whether it's a piano in a living room or a rock or statue in a garden. It is important to have places or things that encourage quiet and contemplation, as well as acting as devices to slow down fast-moving qi.

Sound

The most common way sound is used in feng shui is with wind chimes. Their gentle song is a sign that stagnant qi is being activated. They can slow qi down if it travels too quickly through a house or deflect sha qi both inside and outside the home. Wind chimes also act as a subtle alarm to let you know when someone's coming, as they react to subtle air movements.

Water

Water represents life and good fortune and, where possible, it should be used for the positive energy that it brings. Moving water, like fountains and bubbling aquariums, can help stimulate qi but also have a calming effect because of its cool and passive qualities.

*U*sing the Tools of Feng Shui

The Bagua

*T*HE BAGUA IS A PRACTICAL WAY OF APPLYING THE PHILOSOPHICAL PRINCIPLES OF THE *I CHING* OR *BOOK OF CHANGES* TO FENG SHUI. SHAPE HAS AN EFFECT ON THE FLOW OF ENERGY AND BALANCE AND SO THE BAGUA, USED LIKE A MAP, CAN BE APPLIED TO YOUR PLOT OF LAND, YOUR HOUSE, YOUR ROOMS AND EVEN YOUR FURNITURE.

The bagua represents the eight directions – the eight trigrams of the *I Ching*. Each of these represents the eight life situations – prosperity, fame, relationships, creative energy, travel and helpful people, career, knowledge, and family and health – with the taiji (tai chi) in the middle, represented by the yin/yang symbol of complementary opposites.

You will sometimes find the bagua represented as an octagonal shape and sometimes in the square luo-shu.

For many centuries the Chinese have consulted the I Ching *or* Book of Changes *to give insight into situations in the same way other cultures have used Tarot cards, horoscopes or runes. The key to the* I Ching *are trigrams which indicate degrees of yin and yang as well as the idea of constant cyclical change – the eight stages of life. The octagonal shape of the eight trigrams with unbroken lines (—) representing yang and broken lines (– –) representing yin is called a bagua.*

Using the Bagua

By placing the bagua over a plan of your home or room you can identify your own particular problem areas then set about balancing them. You can activate the relationships corner of your home or your bedroom if you are single and looking for a partner, or place your cash register in the wealth area of your business premises or shop in order to increase profits.

FRONT DOOR

To apply the bagua effectively you will need a plan of your house drawn to scale – graph paper makes it easier – and you will need to find the center and the front (see pages 18–19). The "front door" is where the qi enters your block of land, home, office or room, and its position will help you determine how the bagua should be placed. The front door will always fall in one of three areas, depending on whether your door is in the center (career), to the right of center as you are facing it (travel and helpful people) or to the left (knowledge and intuition).

Few houses or rooms are perfectly square, so by superimposing the bagua over your plan you can identify the problems associated with unusual or unbalanced shapes. A missing corner could indicate particular difficulties. If it's the career corner, for example, it could mean problems with work; if it's the health corner it could be ongoing illness.

FRONT DOOR

Any of the general cures – like mirrors, wind chimes or crystals – can be used to make your adjustments and they are interchangeable. If you are having financial problems you would pay attention to the wealth corner of your home. You might put a fish tank there – which in itself represents money – or you could hang wind chimes or a crystal. Your financial difficulties may be associated with your job so you would be wise to check your career corner too.

Mingua or Destiny

As well as working out the ideal feng shui site in terms of being on the sunny side and halfway up a hill, you can also calculate your mingua (ming kwa) or trigram of destiny to determine your most auspicious ji-wei (jee way) or orientation. If your site isn't facing your most favorable direction, you are able to make adjustments to improve your good fortune.

Once you have found the orientation that is most beneficial for you, you can then find your four lucky and four unlucky directions which you can apply to your land, home, rooms or furniture.

Your Best Orientation

Finding your ji-wei involves a simple calculation. You will need to consult the Chinese calendar on page 79 to determine your year of birth. The Chinese New Year falls on different dates in different years. If you were born January 20, 1971, for instance, you would take 1970 as your year of birth because the Chinese New Year didn't begin that year until January 27.

A person's sex also plays a part in determining the ji-wei so the calculation works differently for a man and a woman.

Calculating Your Ji-wei or Auspicious Locations

There are two types of ji-wei, the Xi-Si-Ming (si si ming) which favors westerly directions and the Dong-Si-Ming (doong si ming) which favors easterly directions. The calculations are different for men and women.

If you are a man, subtract the last two digits of your birth year from 100 and then divide by 9. If the resultant number is 1, 3, 4 or 9, your most auspicious orientations are the east, southeast, south and north. If the number is 2, 5, 6, 7 or 8 your most auspicious orientations are the west, northwest, southwest and northeast.

If there is no resultant number you take the number 9. If the number is 5, take the number 2.

Example: for a man born in 1952:

100 − 52 ÷ 9 = 5, therefore take the number 2.

If you are a woman, subtract 4 from the last two digits of your birth year and divide the result by 9. If the resultant number is 1, 3, 4 or 9, your most auspicious orientations are the east, southeast, south and north. If the number is 2, 5, 6, 7 or 8 your most auspicious orientations are the west, northwest, southwest and northeast.

If there is no resultant number you take the number 9. If the number is 5, take the number 8.

Example: for a woman born in 1952:

52 − 4 ÷ 9 = 5, therefore take the number 8.

The number 5 is associated with the center which doesn't have its own forecast. That's why, if, after making your calculations, you have a 5 and you are a man you take the number 2 and if you are a woman you take the number 8.

Your mingua number identifies you as either an Eastern or a Western Life (see next page). In an Eastern Life, a front door that opens towards the east has the most auspicious forecast. In a Western Life, a front door opening towards the west is best.

Mingua Numbers and the Elements

Once you have calculated your mingua number, you can use it to determine your own personal lucky and unlucky directions. It is also associated with the elements which you can then use in their many forms (see page 69) to adjust and balance the unlucky areas of your land, home, room or placement of furniture.

Number	Mingua	Element
1	Eastern	Water
2	Western	Earth
3	Eastern	Wood
4	Eastern	Wood
6	Western	Metal
7	Western	Metal
8	Western	Earth
9	Eastern	Fire

Using the Mingua

Superimpose the center of your mingua over the center of a plan of your home. You will need a plan drawn to scale so it's probably best to use graph paper. You will also need to find the center (see page 18).

Hold the north point of your mingua to the north of your plan to work out which are your lucky and unlucky directions. You can then work on balancing the areas that need attention using feng shui cures.

The simplest method to apply to your own home or room is the square luo-shu. It can also be represented in an octagonal bagua shape or as a compass. If you are a Western Life, for example, your best directions are west, southwest, northwest and northeast. Eastern Life has east, southeast, south and north.

Eastern Life

NW	N	NE
6	**1**	**8**
7	**5**	**3**
2	**9**	**4**

W — E
SW — S — SE

Western Life

NW	N	NE
6	**1**	**8**
7	**5**	**3**
2	**9**	**4**

W — E
SW — S — SE

lucky directions

unlucky directions

Whose Number Do You Use?
Traditionally you would use the calculations of the breadwinner of the household but that isn't always straightforward these days. You can give each "breadwinner" a particular part of the house – one can take the front door and the other the master bedroom. When you have conflicting readings – some lucky and others unlucky – you can introduce colors and objects associated with the appropriate elements to improve the readings. If a member of the household is requiring special attention, for instance an expectant mother, you may choose to adjust the home for her well-being.

Balancing with the Elements

To improve the feng shui in your home, garden or business, you can introduce materials, colors, shapes and objects that correspond with your personal number and element into unlucky areas. If your house is an irregular shape you can also use the elements to balance it.

Take the element that corresponds with your mingua number and mingua direction and see the table opposite for ideas.

A person with a mingua of 8 would have the element earth, and would introduce associated materials, colors and shapes into the unlucky or missing areas.

Wood

- Wooden furniture
- Wooden features like paneling and floors
- Paper products like lampshades
- Plants and flowers, both real and artificial
- Floral prints, stripes
- Columns and pedestals, wooden carvings
- Gardens, plants and flowers in artwork
- Rectangular shapes
- Greens and blues

Fire

- All types of lighting, including electric, natural and candles
- Animal products like leather and wool
- Sunshine, light, people and animals in artwork
- Triangular shapes
- Reds

Earth

- Bricks, tiles or other clay products
- Ceramics
- Squares
- Landscapes in artwork
- Yellows

Metal

- Stainless steel, copper, iron, brass and other metals
- Rocks and stones, granite and marble
- Crystals and gemstones
- Sculpture made from metal or stone
- Circles, ovals and arches, round shapes
- White and pastels

Water

- Water features like fountains and fish tanks
- Reflective surfaces like mirrors and glass
- Wavy shapes
- Black, gray and dark blue

A Change of Home

Looking for a New Home

Choosing Good Feng Shui

WHEN YOU ARE CONSIDERING A NEW HOME, LOOK FOR ONE THAT FITS WITH THE NATURAL LANDSCAPE BECAUSE IF YOU EXCAVATE AND BUILD RETAINING WALLS YOU CUT INTO THE LAND'S NATURAL ENERGY. CHOOSE A HOUSE HIGH ON A HILL IF YOU CAN OR THE HIGH SIDE OF THE STREET. IT WILL HAVE MORE PRIVACY, LESS PROBLEMS WITH WATER AND, ACCORDING TO THE CHINESE, WILL BRING MORE PROSPERITY.

Take into account the following where possible when choosing your new home.

- The block should be rectangular (longer on the northern and southern ends).
- If not rectangular, it is preferable that the block be wider at the back than the front.
- Avoid triangular blocks as stagnant qi can gather in the corners.
- An outlook over water at the front, preferably a lake, river, bay or harbor is good feng shui. Being right on the sea isn't considered as good because the sea can be dark and gloomy.

- Avoid a block of land next to a drainage canal because it will be full of unpleasant sha qi.
- Make sure the land isn't closed in by large trees or large homes, because they block qi.
- The ground must be solid. Sandy, wet or sunken ground will be too damp and will generate dead qi. If plants are having trouble growing on the land it is also a sign of dead qi.

Orientation

While the notion of the ideal feng shui site with front, back and left and right sides is universal, there are general orientations which are considered beneficial.

The living areas, with yang characteristics, should face south or southeast in the northern hemisphere and north or northeast in the southern hemisphere. The angle of the sun should be high in summer and low in winter so the sun will penetrate the house and provide warmth and light.

Sleeping areas have yin characteristics and should be on the north or northwest in the northern hemisphere and the south or southwest in the southern. You want these areas to stay cool.

Open up the south-facing part of your home (in the northern hemisphere) and the north-facing part of your home (in the southern hemisphere) with large glass windows and doors – with protective eaves – to capture the sun. At the same time, guard the northern side (in the northern hemisphere) and the southern side (in the southern hemisphere) from heat loss and cold winds with solid walls and smaller windows.

Damaging sha qi comes from the heat of the western sun so use controlling devices like awnings, blinds or shutters on your western windows. Place amenities – kitchen, bathroom, laundry – at the north (in the northern hemisphere) and the south (in the southern hemisphere) and not in the corners of your home.

Renovating

Keeping character

When you plan to renovate or build onto your house it is important the extensions you make are in character with your existing home. It not only gives your home an attractive appearance, it ensures good feng shui.

But your extensions do not have to be in the same shape as the existing building to ensure good feng shui. If you want to do something quite different, make sure the design is compatible with your existing home yet with a distinct separation in character. For instance, a pointed roof shape (fire) will go with a flat roof (earth) because fire burns to ash or earth; a flat roof (earth) will go with a curved roof (metal) because earth gives minerals or metal, and so on (see THE FIVE ELEMENTS, page 10).

On the other hand, if you were to put a pointed roof shape (fire) against a curved roof shape (metal), a destructive order would be created since fire melts metal; and a curved roof (metal) against a tall rectangular roof (wood) would be bad feng shui because metal chops wood.

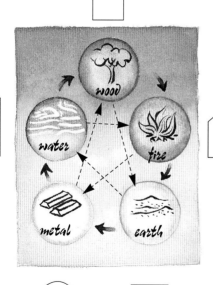

You can use the Five Elements diagram (left) as a guide to ensure that changes to your home follow a productive sequence rather than a destructive one.

It is also important when considering extensions that you take into account the shape of your site and its surroundings.

The Five Elements: The curved, unbroken lines represent the productive sequence; the straight, broken lines represent the destructive order.

Recycled materials

Many people these days use recycled materials – whether for reasons of fashion, to help save the environment or to save money. Take care, though, because renovation should bring new life. You need to be aware of the types of recycled materials you buy and where they end up in your home. Old materials can have "left-over" qi which can affect the feng shui of your home.

There's a general rule – don't use more than one third secondhand materials when you're building.

- Use new material for structural work, like columns and beams.
- Use a mix of old and new in hidden places, like the roof, wall framing or rendered bricks.
- Use new material when on view, like walls and ceilings.
- Always use new materials for plumbing and electrical work.

Secondhand qi
Building materials, antiques and art that have had previous owners can bring bad qi with them. This is when you need more than ever to tune into your intuition. When you are considering buying something that has had an earlier life try to stand very still beside it to determine how it makes you feel rather than how good you think it looks or how much you think it's worth. This will help give you a sense of whether or not it has good feng shui.

Feng Shui Tips and Solutions

*T*HERE ARE THINGS YOU CAN DO, WITH THE HELP OF GOOD FENG SHUI, TO BRING CHANGES INTO YOUR LIFE.

Looking for a Relationship

If you are having difficulty finding a relationship it may be you aren't paying enough attention to the yin or yang (depending on whether you are looking for a woman or a man) in your home. You can make adjustments to your decor to encourage someone to come into your life.

If you are looking for a man, you need to make the left (as you are facing the front) or yang side of your home eye-catching. By drawing attention to this dragon side of the house you are giving yourself the subliminal message you are attentive to men. There's no need to invest too heavily – flowers, paintings or anything bright and cheerful will do. Take care you don't overdo it though – you may find you have more men than you can handle.

Of course, if you are looking for a woman you would brighten up the right side.

Making Amends

When you have had a serious argument with your spouse, tie your two wedding rings together with a red ribbon and put them on your bed head for seventy-two days. The love qi stored in the rings will heal the hurt each night while you lie in bed. If you are not married or don't have rings you can tie two carved wooden turtles (which represent longevity) on the bed head.

Keeping Peace with Your Neighbors

Sometimes conflict with neighbors isn't a case of who's living there but because of the physical layout of the home.

For instance, your living areas which are yang and noisy by nature might run alongside your neighbor's sleeping areas which are yin and quiet. On the other side, your bedrooms might be against the neighbor's driveway which isn't a recipe for harmony. Rituals can help overcome problems like this.

- Try an old-fashioned housewarming party and invite your neighbors to show them your friendly intentions.
- Make plenty of noise and laughter at the party – after all, the neighbors won't complain – to drive out the xiaoren (shiaoren) or little people who have been causing all the trouble.
- Draw these little people on pieces of paper then burn them.

To keep neighborly relationships flowing smoothly, hold these rituals at regular intervals.

Avoid Building Blues

Building a new home is seldom problem-free. The reason for this is that whenever you build you can't help but disrupt the existing qi. Unfortunately it is the new inhabitants who feel the disharmony.

There are three ways to make the process less painful:

- expect to have some difficulties and be patient with builders because they too will be feeling the effects of the troubled qi
- as much as possible, build to fit in with the existing environment and cause less upheaval
- say a prayer of atonement before you start the new work and one of thanksgiving once the work is over.

Being Below Street Level

A front door (and house) below street level means qi can get trapped and business and career opportunities will be lost. One remedy is to install a spotlight aimed at the roof.

Similarly, a downward slope at the back of the house will allow the qi and good luck and money to slip from you. Again, try a spotlight pointing towards the roof, a weather vane, or a tree reaching the roof line.

Outside Obstructions

Obstructions, like a tree or retaining wall directly outside the front door, can block beneficial qi and luck from entering. You don't have to cut the tree down or remove the wall, simply hang a crystal or wind chimes as close to the source of the problem as possible.

Overhead Wires Outside

If you can see overhead wires from your windows it can make you more temperamental – this is the result of the high level of fiery yang qi. Hang a cool jade or ceramic object above your front door to reduce the impact.

Windows and Doors in a Row

Three or more windows or doors in a row will channel qi too fast and cause draughts. To slow it down and disperse it, hang crystals or wind chimes.

Corners and Rooftops

Pointed objects or roof lines can generate destructive qi through your windows. Keep your drapes, curtains or blinds closed at night and hang a bagua-shaped mirror above the window.

Hidden Areas

Attics, closets and basements play a part in the overall feng shui of your home. If you have untidy cupboards it is going to affect the qi around you. Regular spring cleaning is a good idea. Think of it as an exercise in getting rid of bad qi to make room for vital qi or disposing of what you don't use to make space for what's important.

Don't forget to look under the bed. Storing junk there can cause marital difficulties as well as bad health because it encourages qi to stagnate.

Old Year's Resolutions

You can affect your good fortune by carrying incomplete qi from one year into another if you don't finish off any odd jobs that you have already started. It is not a matter of making New Year's resolutions but of tidying up the old one.

A Long Hallway

A long hall or corridor can channel qi – and people – too quickly. To slow things down, try to break your hallway into sections. In a wide hall you can arrange furniture, floor rugs, statues, hall stands and artwork to create a series of separate spaces and points of interest. A mirror at the end of the hallway can help and mirrors placed opposite doorways will open the hallway up and make it seem wider.

Conclusion

Feng shui opens up a whole new world – a new way of looking at and listening to your environment. Once you have this new perspective you can take control of your surroundings, making positive changes to increase your sense of well-being and to improve your health, happiness and success. With the information contained in this book you have the opportunity to create places and spaces that will bring you personal benefits while allowing you to maintain your own sense of comfort and style.

At the end of the day, to feel happy and have a sense of control over your environment means you have succeeded in creating good feng shui.

Glossary

Azure dragon: area to the left of what you are looking at, i.e. a building/house/site, the male element

Black tortoise: protective hill at the back

Chushi (choosi): "out of this world" – psychological feng shui cures

Di qi (te qi): earth qi

Feng shui (fong shwee or foong swee): ancient Chinese theory of design and placement – it literally means (the flow of) wind and water

Huo (hor): fire

Jin (chin): metal

Ji-wei (jee way): auspicious locations

Luo-shu (lo shu): magic square

Ming tang (ming tang): the "bright hall" or the space in front

Mingua (ming kwa): your trigram of destiny

Mu (moo): wood

Qi (chi): universal energy

Red bird: distant front view

Ren qi (ren chi): human qi

Ren tao (ren dao): the way of being human

Rushi (rooshi): "into this world" – physical feng shui cures

San cai (san chie): the three gifts – harmony between a way of life, a place to live and the way of being human

Secret arrows: sharp angles which generate sha qi

Sha qi (shar chi): negative or destructive energy

Sheng qi (shung chi): positive or life energy

Shui (shwee): water

Tao (dao): the "way"

T'u (too): earth

Tien qi (tian chi): heaven qi

White tiger: area to the right of what you are looking at, i.e. building/house/site, the female element

Wu-xing (woo-shing): the five elements or forces of nature

Xiaoren (shiaoren): mythical little people, goblins or imps who gather together in corners where there is dead qi — they cause mischief by gossiping and telling lies

Xue (shu): ideal feng shui spot

Yang: active, masculine qualities

Yin: passive, feminine qualities

The Chinese Calendar

1919	Feb. 1	Ram	1950	Feb. 17	Tiger	1981	Feb. 5	Rooster
1920	Feb. 20	Monkey	1951	Feb. 6	Rabbit	1982	Jan. 25	Dog
1921	Feb. 8	Rooster	1952	Jan. 27	Dragon	1983	Feb. 13	Pig
1922	Jan. 28	Dog	1953	Feb. 14	Snake	1984	Feb. 2	Rat
1923	Feb. 16	Pig	1954	Feb. 3	Horse	1985	Feb. 20	Ox
1924	Feb. 5	Rat	1955	Jan. 24	Ram	1986	Feb. 9	Tiger
1925	Jan. 24	Ox	1956	Feb. 12	Monkey	1987	Jan. 29	Rabbit
1926	Feb. 13	Tiger	1957	Jan. 31	Rooster	1988	Feb. 17	Dragon
1927	Feb. 2	Rabbit	1958	Feb. 18	Dog	1989	Feb. 6	Snake
1928	Jan. 23	Dragon	1959	Feb. 8	Pig	1990	Jan. 27	Horse
1929	Feb. 10	Snake	1960	Jan. 28	Rat	1991	Feb. 15	Ram
1930	Jan. 30	Horse	1961	Feb. 15	Ox	1992	Feb. 4	Monkey
1931	Feb. 17	Ram	1962	Feb. 5	Tiger	1993	Jan. 23	Rooster
1932	Feb. 6	Monkey	1963	Jan. 25	Rabbit	1994	Feb. 10	Dog
1933	Jan. 26	Rooster	1964	Feb. 13	Dragon	1995	Jan. 31	Pig
1934	Feb. 14	Dog	1965	Feb. 2	Snake	1996	Feb. 19	Rat
1935	Feb. 4	Pig	1966	Jan. 21	Horse	1997	Feb. 7	Ox
1936	Jan. 24	Rat	1967	Feb. 9	Ram	1998	Jan. 28	Tiger
1937	Feb. 11	Ox	1968	Jan. 30	Monkey	1999	Feb. 16	Rabbit
1938	Jan. 31	Tiger	1969	Feb. 17	Rooster	2000	Feb. 5	Dragon
1939	Feb. 19	Rabbit	1970	Feb. 6	Dog	2001	Jan. 24	Snake
1940	Feb. 8	Dragon	1971	Jan. 27	Pig	2002	Feb. 12	Horse
1941	Jan. 27	Snake	1972	Feb. 15	Rat	2003	Feb. 1	Ram
1942	Feb. 18	Horse	1973	Feb. 3	Ox	2004	Jan. 22	Monkey
1943	Feb. 5	Ram	1974	Jan. 23	Tiger	2005	Feb. 9	Rooster
1944	Jan. 25	Monkey	1975	Feb. 11	Rabbit	2006	Jan. 29	Dog
1945	Feb. 13	Rooster	1976	Jan. 31	Dragon	2007	Feb. 18	Pig
1946	Feb. 2	Dog	1977	Feb. 18	Snake	2008	Feb. 7	Rat
1947	Jan. 22	Pig	1978	Feb. 7	Horse	2009	Jan. 26	Ox
1948	Feb. 10	Rat	1979	Jan. 28	Ram	2010	Feb. 14	Tiger
1949	Jan. 29	Ox	1980	Feb. 16	Monkey	2011	Feb. 3	Rabbit

Copyright © 1997 Lansdowne Publishing Pty Ltd
Sydney, Australia

United States edition published in 1999
for Hallmark Cards, Inc.
by Storey Books, Schoolhouse Road, Pownal, Vermont 05261
Reprinted 1999 (twice), 2000

All rights reserved. No part of this publication may be reproduced without written permission
from the publisher, except by a reviewer who may quote brief passages or reproduce illustrations
in a review with appropriate credits; nor may any part of this book be reproduced, stored in a retrieval
system, or transmitted in any form or by any means – electronic, mechanical, photocopying,
recording, or other – without written permission from the publisher.

The information in this book is true and complete to the best of our knowledge.
All recommendations are made without guarantee on the part of the author, packager
or Storey Communications, Inc. The author and publisher disclaim any liability in connection
with the use of this information. For additional information please contact
Storey Communications, Inc., Schoolhouse Road, Pownal, Vermont 05261.

Henwood, Belinda.
Feng Shui: how to create harmony and balance in your
living and working environment/text,
Belinda Henwood; consultant,
Howard Choy.